Dressed All Wrong for This

flash fiction

by Francine Witte

BLUE LIGHT PRESS ◆ 1ST WORLD PUBLISHING

1ST WORLD
PUBLISHING

SAN FRANCISCO ◆ FAIRFIELD ◆ DELHI

Winner of the 2019 Blue Light Book Award
Dressed All Wrong for This

Copyright ©2019 by Francine Witte

1st World Library
PO Box 2211
Fairfield, IA 52556
www.1stworldpublishing.com

Blue Light Press
www.bluelightpress.com
bluelightpress@aol.com

Book & Cover Design
Melanie Gendron
melaniegendron999@gmail.com

Cover Art
Radiant Light by Melanie Gendron

Author Photo
Mark Strodl

First Edition

Library of Congress Control Number: 2019949466

ISBN: 9781421836393

This book is dedicated to
Mark, my husband,
and to Lori, my sister, who is
watching over me from Heaven.

I also want to thank Meg Pokrass for her
wonderful editorial help on this collection.

ACKNOWLEDGEMENTS

Grateful acknowledgment is made to the following publications in which these works, or earlier versions, previously appeared:

"When There Was No More Water," *Cream City Review*

"Pigeon Radar," *Storyteller*

"Alpha," *Midway Journal, third place winner for annual contest, finalist Best Small Fictions 2018*

"The Girl Next Door," *Madison Review*

"Death Primer," *Pacific Coast Journal, Barbaric Yawp, Concho River Review*

"Pie," *Kentucky Review*

"Husband Weight," *River Styx*

"Rock, Paper," *Passages North*

"The Baby in You," *Alembic, Georgetown Review*

"When He Left Me," *Minnesota Review*

"Horse Name," *Dos Passos Review*

"When Zac, 32, Strolls in IRL," *Pacifica Review*

"One Marriage Later," *Cutbank, Wind Twirls Everything Chapbook*

"Bia," *Kentucky Review*

"Gladys, Pear Woman," *Cutbank, Wind Twirls Everything Chapbook*

"One Day, Mary Sends her Shadow Out to Work," *Passages North*

"Secret," RHINO

"Gum," *Connotation*

"Wedding Cake Farm," *New Flash Fiction Review*

"Mushrooms, for Example," *New Flash Fiction Review*

"My Mother was a Loaf of Bread," *Rogues Gallery, Wind Twirls Everything Chapbook*

"Suzo the Clown," *Wind Twirls Everything Chapbook*

"Joe and Sue Get in the Car," *Rosebud, Wind Twirls Everything Chapbook*

"When Michael Turns Fish," *Passages North*

"Orange," *Hayden's Ferry Review, Cold June Chapbook*

"Mary as a Constellation," *Beloit Fiction Journal*

"Dogmister," *Pacific Review, Cold June Chapbook*

"Best Day," *Karamu*

"Just Like Camp Songs," *Cold June Chapbook*

"A Jolly Day on Route 95," *Panoply*

"Blind Date," *Main Street Rag*

"Easy Come, Easy Go," *Main Street Rag*

"Sarah Decides to Break Up with Herself," *Iconoclast, Harpur's Palate,*
    Wind Twirls Everything Chapbook

"Clownboy," *Spelk*

"Spy Story," *Passages North, Wind Twirls Everything Chapbook*

"Air," *Hayden's Ferry Review, Cold June Chapbook*

"Suddenly," *Lullwater Review, Cold June Chapbook*

"Dog Name," *2 Bridges Review*

"Flag," *Willow Review*

"At Midnight, You Know Nothing," *Cloudbank*

"Breakfast Story," *Meat for Tea*

"Chicken Pictures," *Steam Ticket*

"Piranha Story," *Green Mountains Review,*
    Wind Twirls Everything Chapbook

"Someone Keeps Calling," *Potomac Review,*
    Wind Twirls Everything Chapbook

"Cold June," *Broken Bridge Review, Cold June Chapbook*

"Marooned," *Newport Review, Cold June Chapbook*

"Next Thing She Knew," *Washington Square,*
    Wind Twirls Everything Chapbook

"The Cake, The Smoke, The Moon," *Pidgeonholes*

"Divorce Stew," *Barbaric Yawp*

"Summer Story," *Kentucky Review*

"The Miller's Barbecue," *Quarter After Eight, Cold June Chapbook,*
    Norton Anthology of Microfiction, 2018

Contents

When There Was No More Water,

She became like a fish out of it. Dizzy. Always dizzy. And dry.

She would ready her arms for floating. Let them stretch out long and perpendicular. But nothing. Always nothing.

She thought of how she got here. Days and days of scorching sunlight. And other obvious signs. In fancy restaurants, when conversation turned to global warming, for instance, she said she would rather talk about film.

She said you have to be civilized and not think about natural occurrences. Those things matter to animals. Then she would order pie.

She said there are scientists who study earthquakes and volcanoes with their drooly lava. Don't worry. The scientists will let us know in time. That's what we pay them for.

Then, what we can do is pile into our gas-efficient cars. And if someone is low on gas that day or didn't get to the ATM, well, that's just nature thinning out the herd.

We could pile into cars and move like blood toward a big-heart mountain. The mountain would cleanse us, and then, when it's safe, we could simply flow away.

That's all there is to it, she would insist.

Then she would drink her coffee.

Of course, when there was no more water, she could no longer do that.

Pigeon Radar

One day, Pam loses her pigeon radar. She forgets how to get out of the way. She bumps into strangers at every turn. *I am a stone hurtling through the universe,* she jokes, but no one is amused. They just scowl and check themselves for fruitbruises.

She finally gives up and stays home. Resigns herself to a life of telecommuting and takeout. She also decides to quit men. Too many twists and turns. Instead, she falls in love with the shopping channel.

She orders things like blue satin pillows and rhinestone cushions to line her walls. She covers the windows with foam. Everything fine, until Smith, the nosy cat neighbor, knocks at her door.

"They brought me your Chinese," he says, peeking into her paddy apartment. He looks at the pillows nailed to the wall and asks if she sleeps standing up. "I did that for a year when my wife left," he says. "If it weren't for the cats sprawled across the couch, I would have forgotten how to lie down."

Pam takes another look at Smith and the kindness in his eyes. His hair, black and suddenly touchable. After a moment, she invites him in. They end up making love on her squishy sofa, and when it's over, she feels her pigeon radar coming back.

She is so excited, she wants to grab Smith, run outside, and tell the world about their new-found love. That's when Smith reminds her he only stopped by for a moment, and really, he has to go.

Later and alone, Pam thinks about how quickly she fell, how easily she scuttled into love. And she wonders if there were only some way she could pad the walls around her heart.

Alpha

After watching the nature channel, you decide to go live with the bears. You like their simple simplicity. Mouthsalmon, tree paw, and backscratch. You won't miss the human things, the traffic, the money, or the clothes.

You travel to find an appropriate forest. One with lush foliage and animal stink. You tear off your clothes and stuff them under a mossy rock. You change your mind and float them down a stream.

Before long, you see your first bear. You name him Roscoe, though naming is such a human thing. He leads you to the others. They look at you blankly, heads tilted, but Roscoe nods, and they seem okay. Clearly, he is their alpha.

He takes you aside and shows you how to climb a tree, how to sniff out berries, and dig up twigs. A part of you misses the hubbub of traffic, and your clothes, which are floating in the stream like a chalk outline.

You think it might help to teach him a bit about your culture. You start with money and how, near dinnertime, it can be used to purchase food. Donuts and pizza and hot dogs.

You pick up a leaf. Foldable and green. How very much it looks like cash. You place it firm in Roscoe's paw. You start to think how easy it would be to take over here, become the alpha yourself.

You explain to Roscoe that he would take the money and hand it to someone, and in exchange they would give him food. You are frustrated at first that this poor beast has no idea what you're saying. And then just as you are about to give up, Roscoe presses the leaf into your white fleshy palm, and just before he swallows you in five efficient gulps, you are almost proud.

THE GIRL NEXT DOOR WANTS TO BORROW MY FATHER

She's 13, and there's this camping trip, she says. A lot of the other girls do it. Julie Paterson, whose dad got killed in the mudslide, Paris Abramowitz, who has a couple of spares, if you count her 5 step-dads, but she hates them all, and then there's Barbie Cantwell, whose father, everyone knows, is just a sperm.

I tell her my pops is usually busy. He never is, of course, but she doesn't have to know. "Flying lessons," I tell her. *Flying lessons!* What the hell. Nah, I tell her, I'll give him the message when he gets back. He's out right now doing the grocery shopping.

My father never used to go shopping, but when the mudslide hit, and our house ended up halfway down the hill and just stuck there, he went looking for my mother. He found her in a motel with Mr. Anthony, the grocer.

Before the mudslide, we didn't live next door to the girl who wants to borrow my father. My father liked it that way. No neighbors way up there at the top of the hill. Damn mudslide, my father said after, now we gotta deal with the people.

So when my father gets home, I tell my father about the neighbor girl and how she wants him to go camping. I present it like it's something he wouldn't want to do in a million years — I tell him about marshmallow roasts and tents and lanterns. I tell him there will be other borrowed fathers there.

To my total amazement, my father agrees to go. Tells me it's his duty, really, cause the girl's father was killed when our house slid down on him during the mudslide. By the time the rescuers found him, he was just a pair of workboots sticking out of the mud.

So you see, my father says, I kind of owe her. *We* were the ones who slid into *her* life. Kind of like the way you slid out of my life when your mother took up with *you know who*. When I tell him that it wasn't my fault, that, in fact, I was at school that day, he just says, yeah, but you remind me of her.

When I point out that my mother is still alive, and he is still married to her, he walks outside to the porch and stares up at the near-naked sky. He waits for awhile, and when a dark cloud finally passes overhead, he smiles a little. I can only imagine he is waiting for rain.

DEATH PRIMER

Some of you have asked what it will look like when you are dead. Let me demonstrate by lying down on this cold, slabby marble. Pretend my chest isn't moving with breath. Pretend my closed eyelids don't flutter.

You might wonder why I am lying on my back. You might wonder why no one is ever buried on their side, curled up like a fetus. After all, they are just a baby now in the afterlife. As you can see, the symbolism would be too obvious.

Remember, someone will be by to put makeup on you. Rouge your cheeks, slick back your hair. Some of you will actually look better than you do right now.

The good thing about dying is that you won't have to think anymore. No one will blame you for your bad decisions. No one will ask you where you put the remote.

When news of your death gets outs, someone will shed a tear for you. Someone else will say they saw you last week. Think about the people who will make casseroles for your poor, hungry family. Think of how good you would feel.

Think about everyone you ever knew and what they will be doing when they hear about your accident, overdose, heart attack. They will all have the exact same thought. They will all shake their heads and think they could have been nicer to you. They will probably be right.

PIE

My mama blows in, storm that she is, and says she wants her some blueberry pie. I say, girl, you haven't talked to me in ages. How you gonna come at me like that? She says I'm still the mama in this drama and you, dear girl, ain't shit.

This kind of talk was so much of my childhood, you have no idea. She says if it weren't for her drunken whorin' ways, I never woulda even happened. I'm just what she got for likin' sex and likin' it where and whenever. Couldn't point to my daddy for a million, trillion bucks.

Further, she tells me, she was all tart perfume and mini-skirt and sashayin' her ass into the nearest bar and doin' it in the men's room. Right above the toilet which is where I was probably made.

Then she asks, you gonna get me that pie or what?

Husband Weight

When Mary drops her husband weight, she starts to feel better. Her cheeks get their apples back, and she feels light and airy to the touch.

The husband weight has crept over to Janet, Mary's best friend. It is threatening to climb up under her skin and pouch her up the way it did Mary.

Mary tries to warn her, but Janet's mouth is full of chewy, delicious love. "You don't get it," Janet says between bites. "This is the weight of someone keeping you steady."

Oh, Mary gets it, all right. Didn't she hug that weight around her like a blanket? Didn't she listen as words of love turned into bits of sweet, fat chocolate?

Then one day, Mary overheard a phone call. "It's you I love," her husband was saying, and, "I'm leaving her today." Which he did. Mary tried to stop him, but how could she when she had to struggle side to side just to stand?

Now, Mary is better. Slim and achy with hunger. But this is how she likes it. She decides that Janet will have to figure out the husband weight for herself.

And so, Mary goes shopping. In the store, she breezes by the muu-muus with smug satisfaction. But then, she sees the wedding gowns, gorgeous and buttercream. Something squeezes inside of her. Her eyes sticking on them one beat longer than they should.

Rock, Paper

"C'mon," Smith says, "shoot!"

We are choosing for something important, though I forget what.

I think back to sweet Alan. My first and only fiancé. We had developed a game of fullbody RPS. Rock, you balled up into fetal position. Paper, you lay flat out, and scissor, you cut each other with your legs. We did this at our first burst of love. At first burst, you can do stuff like that.

We would do this to decide what restaurant to go to or who would get to name our kids.

The kids we would never have.

Smith is impatient, "c'mon!"

Oh yeah, now I remember. He wants my office. Says I'm a woman anyway, and I don't deserve it. "Whadja give old Weintraub a 'snow' job?" Smith thinks he's fuckin' adorable.

I should report the hell out of Smith. But he'll get his. One day, he'll pull out his penis at the wrong time, and someone will choose scissor.

I think about Alan again, how he put up with me forever, and in the end, I balled him up and tossed him in the corner. If it were now, I swear I'd let him cut me. I would lie there all flat and paper and not say a word.

"Rock!" I say to Smith, who like a fool has chosen scissor.

"Ha!" I say, "rock tops chop!" I'm not sure if that's even true, but Smith has bought it, and that's all that counts. I wander back to my still-mine office. Sometimes, I think I'm fuckin' adorable, too.

The Baby in You

Strangers stare at pregnant me like it's something they've never seen. They would sooner believe that it's a watermelon under my shirt.

A cashier at the Walmart rings up my bag of *M&M's*. "Does the baby in you allow these?" I look at her, question mark on my face. "I mean," she continues, "you gonna keep these down?"

My mother, who is standing next to me, explains. "She means that the baby in you is the boss now. If she likes it, you can eat it." I wonder if I was ever allowed such luxury when I was in my mother's stomach. My mother never asked if we should leave my father behind, middle of the night like we did when I was five. I would have puked that up bigtime.

The cashier wraps my *M&M's* and wishes me luck. My mother and I walk outside to the parking lot. Cars like schools of parked fish.

"If you had been smart," my mother points to my stomach, "you wouldn't have strangers telling you what to do."

We find her car, which is a rental, just like everything else in her life. "If you had been smart," she continues as I slide into the passenger seat, "none of this would have happened."

Now, I am used to being spoken to like this, but the baby in me isn't and hurls it back up.

"And how smart were you?" the baby in me is making me say, "to have a baby you didn't want with a man you didn't love?"

My mother looks dead ahead and grips the steering wheel. "Why don't you have some *M&M's*," is all she finally says.

I open the bag and pop a handful into my mouth. Then my mother and I wait for a moment to see what will happen next.

Horse Name

Joan asks me what my horse name would be.

"You know, like Twinkles or Pokey," she says. "You know, what they would call you if you were suddenly a horse."

I don't think that's likely to happen. But anyway.

"It can be a characteristic," she says. "Something that's true about you."

"In that case, my horse name is — *takes too long to get out of a relationship*," I say. "That's what's truest about me."

"You got that right." Joan clears her throat, but it sounds like a low horse snuffle, if you ask me.

I've known Joan for what — 20 years? She prattles on and on, and frankly, I haven't listened for ages. Not when she warned me about Harvey. Not when she warned me about Tim.

"You should have —," Joan says. "You should have —." I have tuned her out even now, but really because I am watching her shake her head, mane-like. At this point, Joan goes silent and begins to stomp her hoof, and she noses towards a saddle I hadn't noticed before.

"You want to go for a ride?" I ask. "Is that it, Girl?" Well, it's not like I can call her Joan anymore. And she never did tell me what *her* horse name would be. Which, to tell the truth, is information I really could have used.

WHEN HE LEFT ME,

I went circle. Lost my shoulders and folded into a ball. I rolled around the living room. I turned bruisey and blue as I bumped up the couch. I got splinters from the unpolished floor.

When he left me, I went rectangle, square, and then rectangle. I was trying to fit the shape of my bed.

When he left me, I went triangle. A single point where my head used to be. The bottom was a pyramid base, all open and wide for his return.

When he did return, I went polka dot. I blew in the wind of the left-open window. Soon, I went glitter all over the floor. He thought for a moment to clean up the mess, but scooped up a handful and walked to the door.

WHEN ZAC, 32, WALKS IN IRL,

he looks nothing like his profile pic. For one, he's wearing a fake moustache. For two, his hair is blonde.

He recognizes me, of course. I've gone to great lengths to look exactly like my profile pic, which is me in my cooking class, and I'm sitting here with a frying pan, just to be safe.

He sits down and explains his disguise. My wife has spies all over, he says. This is the first I've heard of a wife, but whatevs. With my track record, we won't make it past coffee.

I tell him I think he looks better without the moustache, and frankly I thought he'd be taller. He says I look like an idiot, sitting here with a frying pan. It makes me look too wifey, and he's already got one of those.

"I know, stupid, you just told me," I say, and with that, he just pulls out his phone, right there, like I've gone invis.

I hear the beep on my phone and figure what the hell.

I see it's a message from Zac, 32.

"Hi beautiful," it says, "what are you up to?"

"I miss you," I type in, "like you wouldn't believe."

One Marriage Later

Julie says, "what's another word for love? Six letters."

Jack has no idea, having just tipped the bellboy a hundred dollars by mistake.

The same palm trees outside the same Caribbean window. "I thought this would be different," she sighs.

"I heard," Jack says, "that a hundred bucks is like a thousand down here." He picks up the phone and presses O.

"What's another word for liar, cheater, thief?" Julie says, squeezing now into a too-tight bikini.

Totally unaware, Jack fumes on hold. Bach concerto or Olivia freakin' Newton-John.

"You know," she says when the bra doesn't close, "I really hoped this would fit." She tugs and tugs at the lycra spandex. She rearranges her breasts. Finally, she gives up and goes back to her puzzle. "What's another word for another word?"

Jack finally speaks to the phone. "Your bellboy" he says, "I just got robbed."

BIA

She says, as in my life story. As in bio. Only I'm female.

Oh I get it. Got the female part when she entered my office. Bare summer legs. Thighs sturdy as tree trunks.

Where did it start? I ask her. This bia of yours.

Well, she says, my parents met on the internet.

Not that far back, I say. The air smells like her perfume. Like apple. Like something I want to bite.

All right, she says, moving her tree trunks under her mini-skirt. Ten minutes ago, I bought this coffee. Now I'm here.

I like her. Want to hire her. But I future-see where this is headed.

Give me something in-between. Like where you went to school. What qualifies you to work here.

Vassar, she says. I take breaths on an ongoing basis. And I see no other applicants.

She is quite correct. Word must have spread about the difficult interview questions.

I take another look at her tree-trunk thighs. Take another whiff of apple.

I hire her then and there. Let's get back to your bia, I say. What website did your parents meet on?

GLADYS, PEAR WOMAN,

near 50, wants to break every mirror she sees. She wants to, needs to stop looking. Harry, who is only a photograph now, once told her she was made of legs and moonlight and red, red love.

Since then, children and diets and un-diets, till now Gladys sits all day in front of the television. On the shopping channel, tents and tunics to turn her into a secret. Gladys orders one in every shade.

One day, delivering them, the doorman offers Gladys a smile. Ancient reaction — Gladys is smitten, and later, she orders a rowing machine. *How many pounds*, she wonders, *are standing between me and love?*

When it arrives, she rows and rows till her living room is an ocean.

Her daughter begins to complain. "You haven't seen the baby in weeks," she tells Gladys. To which Gladys answers, "I was busy giving birth to myself."

Finally beautiful again, she and the doorman have dinner. Gladys picks olives out of her salad. She scans the menu for fat.

The doorman sparkles like silverware, and when dessert arrives, he spoons cherry vanilla into Gladys' mouth. They plan their second outing, a wine tasting, and when the doorman opens his wallet to pay the check, Gladys pretends not to see the picture of his wife.

Later, hungry goodnight kiss, and Gladys fumbling to open the door.

"I know all your secrets," the doorman says into her skinny ear and turns the key with a flick.

Once inside, they make slithery love on the carpet, her tiny dress flung across the rowing machine. It is only later, when it's over and the doorman gone, that Gladys remembers his wife, thin as a picture, sitting all day in a wallet right there, in front of his heart.

One Day, Mary Sends Her Shadow Out to Work

It starts that morning with snooze and press and snooze again. A half hour later, Mary's shadow is the only part of her willing to move.

This works well for a week or so. It is a deep, snowy December, and Mary likes to burrow under her blankets each day as her shadow tumbles itself into the shower, puts on its shadow clothes, and goes to the office in Mary's place. Everything fine till Mary finds out that her shadow is trying to steal her job.

Mary tries to reason with her shadow. "Look," she says, "I will still let you follow me." But it's too late. Her shadow has tasted freedom, and that's just that.

Next morning, Mary goes back to the office, and there it is under bright fluorescent, Mary's shadow already at the computer. Mary goes straight to her boss, who turns out to be no help. "Business is business," he says. "Besides, your shadow doesn't take a coffee break."

Later that night, Mary goes home to find her shadow in bed with her boyfriend. When he looks at Mary from the corner of his eye, he tells her that he's sorry, but her shadow never turns him down.

What else can Mary do but wait for the next moonless, lampless night? And when it comes, Mary knows she has to sneak herself out of town. In the pitch black, she throws shirts and socks into a suitcase and tip-toes her way down the stairs. She gets into her car and drives beamless towards the highway.

Everything fine till the highway lights, hovering like tall aliens in the near distance. And just as Mary thinks about turning back, there it is — her shadow — beside her in the passenger seat. Black and turning blacker in the sudden bleach of light. And before Mary can even speak, her shadow has edged itself behind the wheel, forcing Mary to move aside.

"Relax," her shadow says in its sudden, shaky voice, "I'll do the driving from now on."

SECRET

Don't tell, Mama says when I catch her eating the chocolate cake in the middle of the night. Your daddy, he don't need to know. Just gonna make him fret.

My head is a lake. All kinds of boat secrets floating around. Some of them sunk to the lake floor.

I tell Mama, don't worry. Why, just last week, I spent all morning eating the bananas off the stand at Carter's grocery. Just stood there like a burglar monkey.

I don't know why she's hiding things from Daddy, him being all dead like he is.

We go on like that, me and my mama. The air filled with deadness and chocolate and secrets in the quivering dark.

GUM

When Buster asks Ginny for gum, she shrugs and gives him the piece right outta her mouth.

"Eww," he shrieks, little-girl style, "you're icky!"

Ginny knocks Buster over, sandcastle-style and moves on.

"Where are the exciting men?" she asks the windrumble as it whooshes by. "The men who will toss me around like you."

The wind just scatters her pile-of-leaves style and moves on.

Later, she gathers herself and pops a fresh stick of spearmint into her gumhole. Gnaw and crackle and grind. And then, she meets Greg.

He is all leather jacket and body spray. Eyes that could smoke her down to a stub.

Ginny quits everything, including the gum, because everything bothers Greg. She misses the gum most of all, because she isn't quite sure what to do with her teeth. In the end, she just lets them rot out.

Which isn't the best decision. Turns out, Greg doesn't care for a toothless woman, and will, in time, end up scraping Ginny off of him, gum-on-your-shoe style.

WEDDING CAKE FARM

Uncle Astor had a wedding cake farm. Aunt Lula was against it at first. Folks don't want a cake from out of the ground, she said. But Uncle Astor proved her wrong.

No, he said, folks like when it springs fully formed right out of the dirt. All fondant and buttercream. Leaves them time for flowers and photographers.

He just had to point her to the line all the way from the barn to the edge of the property. Bride after bride shaking dollars in their fists.

And happy they were when they left the barn with their arms full of perfectly-tiered cake mountains. Sugar flowers growing on top.

Aunt Lula came around to nodding her head. Good crop, she would say to Uncle Astor.

Till one day, she follows her gut to the highway, where smack in the middle she sees a brideless cake, cars and trucks veering around. She sees a line of tears that lead to Mitzi McCall sitting at the edge of a cool pine forest, herself pulled into a tiny ball.

Aunt Lula looks past Mitzi to discover a grove of wedding cakes like little sugar bushes.

"Who the hell wants a dirt cake?" Mitzi finally sniffs to Aunt Lula, who pulls up a bit, happy to be right, after all. "And no one warns you till too late," Mitzi continues, "how your man will leave you just like that when he sees this is the kind of bad decision you are likely to keep on making."

Mushrooms, for Example

Mildred never cared much for them. Says they are too much like men, and you can't always smell the poison. So when her best friend, Jen, waves a Portobello under Mildred's nose, she can't help but turn away.

"You promised to try," her best friend, Jen, says. "It's because you're jealous of me, right?"

Mildred knows this is a beehive. One wrong poke, and all that.

"Who wouldn't be jealous of you?" Mildred smiles. "Your beauty, your cooking skills?"

"Then eat," her best friend, Jen, demands.

Mildred takes a grimace-y bite. *It's a tangerine*, she says inside her head. *Or better yet, a fingerling potato, a tender juicy steak.*

Her best friend, Jen, is watching Mildred carefully, twirling a stray strand of hair the way Mildred hates.

"This is delicious," Mildred says, her mouth still full of mushroom.

"Then swallow," Jen says. "I've got all day."

Mildred thinks back to the other times Jen got what she wanted. The cutest pup from the neighbor's litter, the calfskin purse Mildred had her eye on. And then, of course, Mildred's husband, Harry.

Mildred sits there, not so budgy this time. No, this time she will chew and chew all night if that's what it comes down to.

MY MOTHER WAS A LOAF OF BREAD

Before she had me, of course. Twisted, braided challah loaf, egg sheen on her back. She met my father in a restaurant, *Sam's Old-Time Deli*, on Orchard Street. He was about to tear off her voluptuous elbow when she cried out in fear.

My father was startled a little. Challah had always been silent. But then he thought maybe this one has something to say.

He smuggled my mother out of there. A waiter who smelled mostly like onion was giving him a shifty eye. Wouldn't you like a doggie bag, Sir? he said in his mostly onion way. To which my father said, I ain't got a dog.

Later, my father sitting in Washington Square, my mother next to him on the bench. The afternoon sun baking them both a little bit more. My father liked her bready smell and said she reminded him of his childhood in Brooklyn, his mother's kitchen, speckled black roaster pans and juicy chicken.

My mother responded mouthless, said she liked his gallant way. How he spoke up to the nosy waiter. How he didn't send her back for a quieter bread.

Six months later, she was human. Something happened there that they both felt I was better off not knowing. They do have pictures though of her before it happened, when she was still a challah. My father holding her high in both hands, his eyes and mouth wide open in obvious jest, about to take a bite.

Suzo the Clown

I remember him from my birthday party. I was nine, maybe ten. My father had gone back to drinking and had met some pretty weird characters at the *Half Moon Bar and Grill.* Suzo and my father spent Thursday nights trying to outdrink one another. Suzo always lost, and that's how my father got him to entertain for free.

Suzo didn't wear clown makeup or clown shoes. He was more of an emotional clown. He got us in a circle and told us about his wife, Methuselah. How he drove her up Shaw Mountain and left her there as bear food. He thought that was pretty funny.

When Suzo told this story to my little party friends, we got really scared. Is this what we can expect from men when we grow up? And just as we started to wring our hands, Suzo's wife showed up, driving into our living room in her little clown car. Then she piled out with Suzo's other ten wives. None of them bear food after all.

My party friends and I ate our cake and giggled as Suzo's wives ran after Suzo in a crazy, meat cleaver conga line. We really got a chuckle out of that.

JOE AND SUE GET IN THE CAR

"Fix it, you gotta fix it," Sue says. "Goddamn springs sticking in my ass."

"Just like you," Joe says.

They are too young to be fighting like this. Too much in love, their friends would say. Barb and Jim would swear this over apple-tinis.

The car heads towards the mall. Drives itself, you might say. Joe would rather blind his eyes than see this road again. How many blendertoaster thing-a-ma-jigs does a human person need?

Sue hears this thought and stops applying her lipstick. "If you'd stop breaking the china," she says, "we wouldn't need to replace it."

"I was perfectly happy without china," Joe slams back.

"Sure, sure," she smacks her perfect lips together. "You'd be happy eating off of paper all your life."

"What did I ever see in you?" Joe pulls into a parking spot, and the car goes silent underneath them.

"I think we were very lonely," she says.

"I think we are lonely again," he says.

For a long moment, quiet and then, "I used to put this lipstick on for you," she says.

A car pulls up behind them, shark-like. Coming or going, the driver wants to know. Joe looks at Sue, her pink lips pouting, the springs poking her through the worn-out vinyl.

She gets out of the car and heads towards the mall. Joe watches her and turns on the ignition. He backs out of the spot and signals to the driver, ready and waiting to take his place.

July

100 degrees, and when you ask Reynaldo what happened to his wife, he starts to zipper shut. You change the subject. "Do you like the Ferris wheel at the amusement park?" you say, trying to be light and funny. "They don't let you on without a partner."

"I killed her, okay?" Reynaldo says, his face flush behind the five o'clock shadow.

"Well, you must have had a good reason," you say, determined to salvage the moment.

"No," he says. "It was a ruthless act. I am not at all proud."

You like this about Reynaldo — his lack of melancholy and remorse. So refreshing after the bubble-wrap geeks you are used to.

Later that night, you shimmy over to the amusement park. You intend to keep this thing going and head straight for the Ferris wheel.

"Tell me, Reynaldo," you say, "if I were to fall, would you try to catch me?" You see the zipper closing again. You have clearly struck the wrong chord.

You move up three spaces in the line, and that's when you see a young woman falling from the top of the Ferris wheel, her legs in flowered tights forming a victory V.

"That's how my wife died," Reynaldo says, his hand urgent, pushing at the small of your back. The thinnest film of sweat forming there having nothing to do with July.

WHEN MICHAEL TURNS FISH,

h e doesn't understand. He is clueless in the conference room, fiddling with his slide presentation. His brain flipping and flapping in the waterless air.

As his skin scales over, he is thinking of Margaret, his wife. How she will never accept him as fish and might just run off with Gustav, her guitar instructor, who after one whole year has only taught her three chords.

As his arms tuck in and he is left with fins, he drops the projector remote, and no one even offers to pick it up.

And he doesn't mind for himself, but more for Celeste, who might not enjoy that he has no arms, no hands, and can no longer hold her for long, stroke-y hours on motel Thursdays.

His legs are gone, and there goes his hair. His nose juts forward, and his eyes are on either side of his face. He can clearly see Celeste playing footsie with Clark from Legal.

And it's just as well when he tries to speak but his mouth just opens and closes and opens and closes and nothing comes out, because what does he really have left to say?

And is that Gregor, the summer intern who went on and on about wanting a job exactly like Michael's? Is he really standing over there in the corner right now wriggling a worm onto a hook?

ORANGE

Marilyn liked orange things. Thought orange was a happy color and so full of Vitamin C. "Look," she would say whenever she wore her orange dress, "don't I look nutritious?"

Soon, she met Bentley, a car salesman in need of a wife. He liked Marilyn's sunny orange attitude and proposed on their very first date.

Her wedding gown was orange, of course, and designed to poof out in sections so it looked like she was wearing a tangerine. Bentley was so impressed, he vowed to love this nourishing woman who would fortify him all of his days.

They honeymooned in Florida, and she insisted they move there. He wanted to protest, but she gave him her sunniest smile, and he sent for his cars the very next day. When the cars arrived, Marilyn painted each one a deep, screaming orange. It was such a blinding sight that the customers had to wear sunglasses on top of their sunglasses. And since nobody even wanted an orange car, Bentley ended up going broke. Marilyn assured him it would all work out. They were living mostly on oranges now and were, therefore, easy to feed. Again, he wanted to protest, but remembered that it was her happy orange attitude that had made him fall in love.

Then, one afternoon, Marilyn decided to paint everything in the apartment orange, including the chair Bentley was sitting in. Rather than have him move, she brushed the paint right over him. "You know," she said, stepping back, "I kind of like you this way."

He said nothing, but a tiny part of him was starting to be unhappy.Later that evening, Bentley sat silent in his orange chair. Now that he was the same color as everything else, Marilyn could no longer find him. She called out his name and patted the chair he was sitting in, but he said nothing.

She called and she called but still no answer. And even though the sun had gone down, it was still orange daylight inside and bright enough for Marilyn to keep looking. All the while, Bentley, sitting right there in the open, a mute orange stone.

MARY AS A CONSTELLATION

When Jim told Mary to get her naggy self off the planet, she took him literally and became an astronaut. She suited up, threw on her oxygen tanks, and zipped into the stratosphere.

When she got to Neptune, she took out her telescope and looked down at Earth. She could see Jim with his new love, Amelia. She couldn't hear them, of course, but she could tell by Jim's hand gestures that he was bragging about sending Mary into outer space.

"That bastard," she echoed into the cavernous dark. "Here I am, floating like a stupid moon while he does the moving on thing."

Mary tried to think of clever things she would say to Jim when she got home. But all she came up with was "how dare you" or "I'll get you for this."

Eventually, her throat got tired and besides, she had the feeling that even the universe was sick of her endless complaints. That's when she took a good, long look at the white, sashy galaxy, the twinkly stars lighting up all around her.

And she decided that from now on, she would stay where she was appreciated, and that Jim would need a telescope and a clear, moonless night if he was ever going to see her again.

DOGMISTER

My new boyfriend is a dog. And not a metaphor dog. And not in a bestial way. We have no intention of sex. Sex is for the human/human and dog/dog pairs.

No, it's more like this. He's a collie terrier mix and, therefore, prefers the *New York Times*. He comes over Sunday morning. I have bagels and kibble spread out — a brunch buffet. I say, "Dogmister, you are so very special. It's a shame we have to hide our love."

He simultaneously wags his tail and says, "Yes, it is a damn shame." When I ask about the tailwagging, he says, "it's a hard habit to break."

Dogmister goes on to read me the book review, so I don't have to strain my human eyes. Dog eyes can see in the dark, and let's not even talk about the hearing part.

Later, Dogmister says it's time to go, but that I look lovely, and he'll call me when he gets home.

Which he never does, but I always end up forgiving him anyway.

Best Day

Say it's the best day you ever had, and by 10 a.m., you are sitting in the glorious park, and the white magnolias are in perfect bloom. And that's when you notice these two old fedora guys tossing potato chips across the "stay off the grass" grass. They are trying to see who owes who a lunch of baked beans and green peppers, cause there's so little left that farting is all they have. And instead of being amused, your best day starts to turn into some future glimpse freak show.

And that's when you call up your girl, who says she's been sitting there just waiting for something to happen. The acting thing didn't take, at least not in the way she planned, and she just finished a gig as the "K" in supermarket at the opening of the new *Piggly Wiggly*.

And you want to say that that's not even being a real actress, but you don't, cause you know you're not real at what you do, either.

So when she tells you how bored she is, even right this second, you break up with her, but only in your head. And this best day of yours is really starting to suck, and you wonder how you even thought it was a good day in the first place.

And that's when your headbubble mumbles something about the waitress who smiled and served you those voluptuous, syrupy pancakes, and if you had known it wasn't the start of anything, but just another come-on, you might have at least stayed there for a second cup of coffee.

Just Like Camp Songs

Maria likes to hear sweet words of love. Says they make her feel warm and so connected. Whenever a man tells her she is special, well, that's just *Kumbaya* and a campfire.

She has unremembered the scarred marshmallows, their blobby white insides dripping from sticks. Or the showers of sparks coming at her face.

Right now, she is listening to Rico, who promises to leave his wife. He has brought Maria to a secret restaurant where the candles are kept low.

Once I am Rico's wife, Maria thinks, *he will take me to a famous restaurant where crowds of people will see us.*

Just then, the waiter brings their dinner, which in this light, is barely visible. Maria bends down to sniff her plate. Rico tells her he can't see her, but she is so beautiful, she is sending music into the air. The waiter, always one to know where the tips are, asks them if they'd like to sing along.

A Jolly Day on Route 95

I'm filled up with pancakes, and that's when Harry decides to lay the divorce thing right at my feet. *Get outta the car* is what he says.

I slam the door, and he guns the motor. Squeals the car into reverse and turns on the headlights even though it's dead-ass noon.

I'm frankly glad to be free of this loser, and I decide to go back for more pancakes. I don't have to be slim anymore, and also, I don't have to watch what I say.

I'm gonna get fat and tell the next man I see how wrong his mother is about everything, and that the wallpaper in the hallway sucks.

Then I'm gonna waddle myself out to the highway, sleep with a couple of truckers and have them take me out and buy me even more pancakes.

My life is gonna be a road trip. I won't even need a goddamn map.

But, oh, will you look at that? Here comes Harry, his own sorry self, pulling into the parking lot, and me with nothing but pancakes and freedom on my mind. And who the hell does he think he is, treating me like a two-dollar yoyo? That's the first thing I'm gonna ask when he stops all that honking and opens the door for me to climb back in.

BLIND DATE

Jill is halfway to the restaurant. She is all riverflow and deep, cleansing breath. Always been this way. When she found out there was no Santa Claus, it was an icy cool of relief.

Jim is halfway to the restaurant. Nothing can calm the stutter of his heart. Beating like wings, it is. When he found out about Santa, his heartpatter almost floated him away.

Almost there, Jill admires the sunset. Gold and pinks buttering the sky. One with nature, she is. When she was young, she tried to stop a wave mid-curl to ask why it was so angry.

When Jim sees the sunset, his dangerbrain kicks in. Almost late, he puttputters in his head. When he was young, he learned to ignore the ocean, all that back and forth of the tides.

A minute from the restaurant, Jill presses her reflection into a lipstick mirror. Nothing but nose and mouth. Nothing but even breath and words waiting calmly on her tongue.

A minute from the restaurant, Jim is plotting the tables. Will a window shine in too much truthlight? Will a corner smack his words against the wall?

But something happens when they both arrive. A cosmic hand flattens them and make them blend. How oddly calm he feels by the way she glides into the room. How oddly charged she feels by the air all around him that dances to the beat of his butterfly heart.

Easy Come, Easy Go

Harry's favorite thing to say when he's eaten the last of the pie. But me? I was the one who rolled out the dough, pressed the edges inch by inch, and watched the damn thing rise into a fever.

Also, not easy was watching Harry throw his shirts on the floor. The shirts I hand-washed, watched as they bubbled into a wet fabric mountain in the bathroom sink. Waited for the suds to disappear so I could rinse them and wring them dry.

Also, also not easy was watching Harry spread out on the bed each night like a sleepy starfish struggling for air. He motioned me to a spot on the floor. The wood was cold, and I became a blur of myself, smudged like I was among the shirts.

And then, Harry started bringing in hookers each night. To help him with falling asleep, he would say. He would further say I do nothing but feed him pie and dress him in half-washed shirts. How on earth could sleep come easy to him?

Of course, he is right. I belong elsewhere. Tomorrow, I will find a place on the map. Somewhere south of here, so the weight of me could fall into it without me even noticing.

Easy go, as Harry likes to say.

Sarah Decides to Break Up With Herself

Her reasons are numerous. Ironclad. She is sick of the trouble she has caused herself. Years of shattered heart pieces, a cataract of tears. Sarah would like to climb out of her skin and head to California.

She starts to make travel plans. Maps and hotel brochures. One overlooks the cool, blue Pacific. Another is feathered with palms. Sarah sits herself in front of the mirror. "I'm warning you," she wags her finger. "You'd better be good."

And she is good, until that evening when Riley Jackson crawls into her life with no more than a wink. They end up in a floozy motel where the heat of cheap love smudges Sarah to the bed. Thoughts fly out of her head and paste themselves to the wall. *What am I doing?* and *what about his wife?* Sarah remembers her warning to herself, but when she struggles to get up, Riley kisses her naked neck.

Later and alone, she can still feel Riley all over her skin. Her heart drops as he evaporates. By midnight, she gives up and showers off what's left.

After, Sarah calls herself over to the mirror. "I warned you," she tells herself. "We're through." Sarah begins to panic. "But my childhood," she says. "I just wanted to be held."

Sarah stops there. She knows she has a point. All those men with their heartless love, Riley with his sweet, achy touch, how they always came so close.

This continues for hours, Sarah arguing with herself. California, childhood, her poor, poor nagging heart. Finally, Sarah lies down on the cloud of her bed, drifts off to a strange, peaceful sleep. And when morning comes, there is Sarah, still on the bed, holding herself in her own arms.

CLOWNBOY

I call up Clownboy to tell him we're through.

I'll notify the press, he says.

I really mean it this time. Outside, the sky is tangy with rain.

Clownboy doesn't care.

He doesn't care because he's got Priscilla now, who used to be my sister, but isn't anymore. We would stay up late nights painting boys onto each other's fingernails, braiding love into each other's hair.

Now, that's just a hunk of junk. Plastic choking the ocean.

You've gone too far this time, Clownboy. I say this to my silent phone. Sandpaper words in my throat.

Next thing, Clownboy is honking up the driveway, in his silly Clownboy truck. He steps outside even though the sky has started a good soppy rain. I can see the drops ping off his Clownboy truck. When they fall on his face, I pretend they are tears.

I pick the present he gave me last Christmas. A jingle bell necklace he found in the trash. When he gave it to me, I hated him a little. He kissed that right out of me, though.

I'm a bigger clownboy than Clownboy could ever be. I put on my necklace and head out, nearly naked, into the rain.

Not Egg

What do you want for breakfast, Mother says. Egg or not egg? Not egg could be anything. So I say egg.

Good choice, she says.

Only choice, I think, but don't say. That's also a good choice.

One time I said "not egg," and she squinched up her lips. Started looking around the kitchen, her eyes landing on our cat. I ran over and grabbed him, "Egg!" I shouted, running into the parlor, "I mean egg!"

Mother is a tower of horrors. Or not.

Sometimes she is so sweet. Making us breakfast, for example. Asking me what I'd like, for example. Other times, the horror times, she is likely to feed our cat to the neighbor's dog, or chase my brother, Bill, out into the naked cold.

Every so often, I stare at the back of Mother's head. It is an oval with hair. It is an egg with hair. When she turns around to look at me, to catch me doing something wrong, her face is the face of an egg with a few holes punched in. The goopy yellow all run out.

Those are the times I really want to say, not egg.

My Other In-Law Sister

It's Friday, which means dinner with the in-laws. Which is strange, because my husband left me years ago.

We have a favorite restaurant. Dark and at the edge of town. Round table, way in the corner. We leave an empty place for my husband.

My first in-law brother orders an extra meal, and we set it at the empty place.

My first in-law sister sets out the toys for the children my absent husband and I never had, but "should have" she winks.

My in-law mother fidgets. She puffs the air and finally says, "in my day, we kept our men with apple pie and negligees."

My other in-law brother tells her, "Mother, you say this every week."

I wait for my other in-law sister to say something. Anything. Wasn't it really her fault in the first place? Didn't she fill up my husband's ear with stories about me and Ernie that were only partly true?

Instead, she has slid into the empty place and begun eating the nearly cold meat loaf that, honestly, my husband would have never ordered to begin with.

And when the check comes, and my first in-law brother shakes his head like he always does, and asks why the hell we are even doing this, my other in-law sister puts a napkin to her gravy lips. "Food's good," she simply says.

SPY STORY

Ginelle was tired of Greg's cheating, and so she hired a spy. When the spy found no immediate evidence, she decided she liked the idea of having her own spy and kept him anyway. She named the spy Hector: a code name, she explained. Then she bought him a fedora.

Hector brought her disturbing reports about fecal matter in drinkable water, impurities in breathable air. And that was just the start.

Soon, Hector began to notice that Ginelle's husband was staying out every Thursday night with no clear explanation. He said that might be worth his attention.

"Never you mind," Ginelle told Hector. "We are doing more important work." Hector returned to his post at the mall. It turned out, just as Ginelle and Hector suspected, that there really was no video surveillance at the ATM.

Greg expanded his Thursday nights into weekends, and soon he was leaving Ginelle messages on the answering machine *Be back Wednesday for socks* or *here's my new address.*

Hector pointed out that these are clear signs of a straying husband. Ginelle said she was tired of Hector's fedora and was thinking about going a little more James Bond. "You'd have to drink martinis," she said and mixed one up for him.

Hector said he would do whatever she paid him to do, but wasn't she worried about her husband?

"What would you charge me to be my husband?" Ginelle asked him squarely.

"I'd have to crunch some numbers, "Hector said, sipping his martini. "I'll get back to you by the end of the day."

AIR

Annabel liked to let the air dry her after a shower. No towel. She was the same when it came to the rain. When Nicholas, her gazillionth boyfriend, gave her an umbrella, she dismissed him as dependent and gadgety.

"What did the cave men do when *they* were wet?" she asked him. He had no answer and sat there crying like all the others before him. She warned him not to use a tissue, that the tears would dry by themselves if he would just give them time.

Then she met Hank, a life warrior, who was locally known for bending small objects in his bare hands. Surely, *he* would know how to handle a little water.

They went on their first date to the reservoir, where Hank bent down and took a deep, facey drink. "Why use a glass?" he said. "You need to be one with the elements." When he let the beads of water linger undried on his chin, Annabel fell madly in love.

They got married and quickly returned all the fancy towels and glassware that their used-to-be friends had given as wedding gifts. All with little notes that said *call us again when you "get it."*

Eventually, they were left with only each other, as everyone they knew seemed so attached to umbrellas and tissues and towels. Then, they agreed that words were useless, as so many of them were wasted, and that cave people did just fine with only gestures and grunts.

They also decided that if they ever needed to have an argument, they would jump into the shower together, get sopping, wringing wet and the winner would be whoever the air would dry off first.

Suddenly

Your apartment goes dark. No explanation. You think about candles and fuses and phones. You call to your husband, your goldfish, the neighbor upstairs.

This is an ink dark, the kind that sandwiches the universe. You begin to hunt. Your hand lands on a transistor radio. Static and low battery when you turn it on. You should know better. This isn't your first time stranded in the dark.

Where is your husband anyway? Sitting on the sofa last time you looked. But that was either just now or last November.

As you move through the dark, your thigh bangs the sofa. A bruise that will bloom in two days, and you won't know what happened. You continue to move. You knock over the table. Glass crash as the goldfish bowl explodes on the floor. You bend over to hear the tiny goldfish scream.

The neighbor upstairs has gone silent. No footsteps creaking the wood. No television hum. You think of your own dead appliances. Your frozen food softening, your microwave, unhurried, at last.

Five minutes in the dark. You realize all that you've lost.

Suddenly, the lights come on again.

Dog Name

Charley asks me what my dog name is. "Like if you were a dog," he smiles, his canine teeth bared.

"I don't know," I say, "Fluffy? Puff Ball?"

"That's way too soft for you," he says. "I was thinking more like Snoopy or Sniff."

I look at him dead-eye in the burnt yellow sunlight striping through the kitchen blinds. "This is what's killing us," I tell him. "You, always thinking the worst of me."

He has the stench of that other woman all over him. I can see on his finger pads where he last touched her. Spots like fingerprint ink.

"What would your dog name be?" I ask, throwing him a Frisbee curve. "Hound, or maybe Fetch?"

He doesn't smile now. Just checks his phone for the umpteen millionth time. Then, he takes it outside for a walk.

Later I will check it for texts. Charley knows that I do this. Silly mutt. He doesn't even bother to delete.

He is right about one thing, though. The two of us dogs, hunting and sniffing. Not even enough sense to wipe the blood off our snouts.

Flag

Janie decides to start her own country, one with no heartbreak. She knows she will need a flag. She meets her vice-president, Ruth, for dinner. Ruth was easy to win over because she was sick of her fifth-floor walkup and figured there would be a mansion involved.

They go to a quaint French restaurant. Janie knows that as head of her own country, she will need to understand different cultures. She orders the Coq au Vin though she has no idea what it is. Ruth simply orders some wine. "Our country will have alcohol in all the water fountains," Ruth says in her newly-acquired decree voice.

"All right," Janie says, "but first we need a flag. I was thinking of red to symbolize all the broken hearts."

"And green," Ruth adds. "For all the money spent on therapy."

The waiter brings the Coq au Vin.

"This is chicken," Janie says. "I thought it would be something more."

"You might also say that about love," the waiter smiles.

By now, Ruth has wandered over to the piano bar and is singing slurry Sinatra.

"We were going to start a country," Janie tells the waiter, who has sat down in Ruth's place. "But my vice-president seems to have other plans."

"Your first abdication," the waiter nods. "I would say this calls for a toast." He goes over and grabs a bottle of wine off a nearby table. "I lied and told them this wine was made from the blood of tiny birds," he winks. "They were happy to send it back."

After a glass, the waiter offers to be her vice-president. Janie declines, explaining that men are not allowed in this country free of heartbreak.

"Perhaps I can convince you with a flag." He pulls the table-cloth from under their plates, magician-style. "The flag of our country would be different," he says. "You don't wave it; you wrap yourself in it, like love." Janie is so impressed, she swears the waiter in then and there.

A moment later, Ruth returns, ready to discuss affairs of state. When she learns there has been a coup, she challenges the waiter to a duel.

"I am honored," he says, "to defend my new country." He picks up a nearby butter knife and ties the flag around him like a cape.

Just then, the bird-wine table signals they are ready for the check. The waiter puts down the knife and excuses himself. Sadly, Janie realizes that he would never put national security ahead of getting a good tip.

Ruth is quickly reinstated, but Janie admits to having some doubts. "I thought my own country would be different, but it's nothing but duels and disappointment. In the end, everything turns out to be nothing but chicken."

"Well, this should cheer you up," Ruth says, leaning in bright and hopeful. "I just heard that this place sells the most delicious wine made from the blood of tiny birds."

At Midnight, You Know Nothing

You are sleep-fogged and grunty. You are a stranger in the bathroom mirror.

Five hours ago, you broke a heart. Left it shiver-cracked in a restaurant. You didn't even eat your pasta. The waiter's face called you a shit.

You drove home and turned on some tunes. Electric Jimi H. When the phone rang, it was the broken heart begging for a second, pathetic chance. You laughed and hung up. Ha, you said to the swimmy Jimi air — that'll teach you to love me.

But really, it happened just the opposite. It was *your* heart that got fractured. Your lover walked out, cool and leathered like a shadow. Even the waiter was falling in love. Then, you ate both plates of pasta.

At midnight, it comes back to you. The ten o'clock wine wearing off. You drank yourself to a fever sleep and now, it's mostly gone.

How will you make it to morning? You consider more wine, another stab at the phone. Not sleeping seems fine to you now. Beside, sleep always looks a little too much like death. Yours arms stretched out like rubber bands. Your mouth a wordless cave.

Just then, the telephone. Your lover calling back. You let the machine take it. You lover's voice fills the apartment. Your wine-brain makes you pick up the phone. But it's not at all what you thought.

Your lover, your ex-lover, wants the name of the waiter. This waiter, your ex-lover tells you, is someone he could really love.

Just past midnight and you still know nothing. You promise to find out the waiter's name. But right now you need sleep. You want to dream that none of this ever happened.

When you wake, you will call the restaurant. Later, you will meet your ex for tea at a place where there are no waiters.

Look, you will tell yourself in the next-night mirror. It is a thread. It will keep you sewn together enough till you figure out your next move.

Breakfast Story

The usual eggs. The usual toast.

The usual space in the bed.

The usual stutter from the dying fridge.

You grab your phone and look up appliance sales. It's time, you think, it's time.

Your husband promised. He really, really promised.

The butter on your toast is curdled. The eggs smell like a night in hell.

Like a night with no sleep. Next to the empty husband space.

Your search brings up nothing. Refrigerators, even cheap ones, apparently, are too handsome for you. You should have learned to eat food that doesn't need attention.

You used to search for your husband's expiration date. He must have kept it hidden behind his heart. Anyway, you keep the bedroom down to freezing, but still it doesn't help.

Your breakfast is rotten, and you know it. The fridge is dying, and your husband is gone. But what can you do? Hunger is a stupid child.

You hold your nose and eat.

THE WOMAN YOU LOVE

The night I leave you forever, I take nothing but a measuring cup. It will remind me forever of the woman you love.

The woman you love probably made you omelets after silky afternoons of whispery romance. Omelets in the afternoon are so wrong, you probably said. Yes, but so delicious, she probably said.

I remember the day the measuring cup showed up in our kitchen. I asked you where it came from and you simply said, a friend. It was nothing special. Pyrex glass, red-lined markings, quarter cup, half cup, full. You probably kept it because you probably poured swirly cake batter from it, probably dotted a touch of it on her probably pretty little nose.

It's three weeks later when I decide to leave. I can't ignore the love pounds on your belly or how you are never hungry when you get home. I ask you if I'm imagining things. You say nothing, but then you walk over and stroke the handle of the measuring cup. You're crazy, you finally say.

I wait until you are sleeping. I hide the measuring cup in my coat pocket and slip out the door. I leave behind my shoes, my books. Nothing belongs to me now.

Later, I sit in the bus station. I am thinking where I can go next. No money, no nothing except the measuring cup with the heat from the woman you love all over it, the smell of your heart coating the glass.

I take off my golden wedding ring and leave it on the bench. Then I place my naked hand inside the measuring cup to see if it can tell me how much of me is going to have any weight in the world.

CHICKEN PICTURES

I feel a kinship with the chickens. Like, I've come from them somehow. The monkey people have it wrong. I *never* feel like swinging from a tree branch. I *do*, however, think about pecking quite often.

And I like that wingy, flapping thing the chickens do when they're angry. Such an efficient way to say, "you are *such* an asshole." I like it so much, I decide to give it a try.

When Smith walks by my cubicle, when he *cockwalks* by my cubicle, his head is jutting ever so slightly forward and back. "Hey Smith," I say, "got a minute?"

He bird-swivels his head in my direction. "I'm busy," he says.

Yeah, I know all about it. On his way to a meeting where he can beak-push some corn kernels at a client, who, in turn, will beak-push alfalfa meal back at him.

"It's *important*," I insist. There I go, pecking again. I pull out my wallet, bulging with chicken pictures. I show him a shot of Frank, a swarthy Rhode Island Red who, I swear, could pass for Smith's twin brother. "Doesn't it bother you that we *eat* these guys?" Now, I know it's gonna piss him off, but maybe Smith will rise to the occasion and say, "I guess we're basically cannibals," or something profound like that.

But true to form, he stands there thrusting his head back and forth, much more noticeably than before. "You know," he says, "you are such a loser." He is clucking wildly now. "You and your stupid chicken pictures!"

Around us, all the nearby heads are poking up and staring out from their coops. And instead of calling him a jerk, like I normally would, I decide to try the flapping thing. I stand up right there and flail my arms, papers whirring about on my desk. Anger in a language only a chicken would understand.

"You don't have to curse," Smith says, as he walks away, without even *admitting* why he is saying it.

PIRANHA STORY

One day, all the piranhas jump out of the oceans. Just like that. By five o'clock, they have flipped and flapped themselves to death on the dry land. Wild dogs eat their fishy flesh. Soon, the piranhas are nothing but bones and razor teeth.

Everywhere, people are happy. No more piranhas, they sing out in glee. One less thing to worry about. Until somebody points out the obvious. What is down there in the ocean to make even a piranha afraid?

First thing, they close the beaches. Divers are hired by the boatload. Lobstermen offer up their traps. Psychics appear on the shorelines, tarot cards in hand.

Days and days go by. The newsman reports nothing new. The floor of the oceans have been scoured, he says. Scoured, like a dirty tub. Maybe, the weather guy jokes, the shrimp will start jumping out. Better get the cocktail sauce!

Finally, everyone relaxes. Piranha-less, the beaches reopen. Jugglers and clowns on the boardwalk. Children plopping wet sand into pails. The first brave man sticks his toe in the water. *Look!* He does a little dance. *The ocean don't throw me out like a shoe!*

One day, the newsman reports an odd rash of dog death. Something they might have eaten, he says.

The weatherman puts on his T-storm frown and shakes his head. Bad day to be a dog, he says.

Someone Keeps Calling

A faraway voice. Like a voice underwater. He says hello. Nothing more. He hangs up. Calls back. His breath is angry, inviting, sexual. He's distant, but intimate. Saying nothing. Saying everything.

This night, this 3 a.m. night, I invite him over. He hangs up, scared. I scared my scary caller. He calls back. Ah yes, we are dancing. We are in love.

I tell him if we met, he would be more than just breath. Again, he doesn't answer. Hangs up and doesn't answer some more. At 5 a.m., dreamy drifting, I am awakened by the phone.

Finally, he speaks. He tells me never. I ask him why. He says if we met, we would be real.

Where then, can this go?

Nowhere, he says, but why does it have to? This is perfect, our whispers, our sighs, all mingled in imagined love. You can't touch it. You can't break it. It just is.

Then we hang up forever. I change my number and throw away the phone.

Next time I breathe, I might think of him. Or not. But life will cool to room temperature. No more 3 a.m., 5 a.m. for me.

Of course, I will start to watch my mail. Pray he hasn't found me. No blank, alluring envelopes. No paper to crumple, like me, with desire.

Cold June

The coldest on record. Here in Maine, temps of teens and twenties becoming the norm. Mavis Farnsworth in a pine green sweater. Makes her look like Christmas, her husband, Tom, says. "*I'd* sure like to unwrap you," he adds with a twinkle. She bakes him sugar cookies instead.

He turns on the little TV, all black and white and rabbit ears. These days, the news is always the same. Words like *freakish* and *ice age* and *end of the world*. The anchorman puts on ear muffs as a joke, but the weatherman says it's not funny.

The weatherman talks about a cooling sun, and predictions of ocean waves freezing mid-curl. Cuts to Florida where the local station shows icy palm trees with shivery fronds. Then, a citrus farmer, puffy cloud breath, screwdrivers open an orange, the fruit inside like broken glass. "My wife just bought a winter coat," he says.

Watching this, Mavis just sighs. She has lived in winter coats all her life. Tom snaps off the TV and comes up behind her. He slips the pine tree sweater off of Mabel's birdy shoulder. "Forget all that," he says. "Nothing but fear and commercials." He walks her towards their patchquilt bed.

Mavis looks at the timer. Twenty minutes left till the cookies are done. She doesn't like to interrupt her day, but figures Tom needs something to do. He dims the light to a dark charcoal. Outside the window, ice beginning to lace the trees. The sun going cold as a stone.

Aquarium

When George asked Mary if she liked fish, she wasn't sure what he meant.

"Like on a plate?" she asked, "with dill?"

"No, no," he laughed. "I mean, to look at. At the aquarium."

She felt embarrassed, but he didn't seem to notice. They rode the long, sinewy F train to Coney Island. There, they gobbled hot dogs and talked about their fathers. It seems that both their fathers were great lovers of the Ferris wheel.

"We can go on it if you like," George said. And they did. Up and up and up. People below began to look ridiculous. Too small for their own bones. Mary started to yell things, knowing they couldn't hear. "Hey Peabrain!" she called down, laughing until she looked over at George who seemed oddly offended. "I wonder what you really think about *me*," he said and was silent after that.

Later, in front of the fish tank, water throbbing the glass, Mary watched the fish mouths open and close, open and close. One seemed to stare right at her. Mary could swear the fish was trying to insult her.

She looked at George and waited for him to defend her honor. Whole minutes went by, and after a while, she started to think that George was taking the fish's side in all this.

MAROONED

When Mary pours her cereal, she finds a note — *Help! I'm stranded!* Thank God, she saw it before spooning it into her mouth.

Mary doesn't question how the note got into her cereal box. Instead, she calls the comments and questions number. Not so much to report, but more to get a replacement.

She is clearly annoyed that her routine has been interfered with. She has things to do, and stranded strangers on some cereal island mean nothing to her. Some poor slob shaking a cornflake tree and smacking open a coconut.

Mary has her own problems. Carl went out a week ago and still hasn't come back.

Better to be stuck alone on a private island, Mary thinks, than to be out here in the open where everyone can see.

SHE STANDS THERE, KIND OF OLD LADY

Swaying to and fro, like a rocking chair, only sideways, and her six grandchildren don't call her today, only five, and when she asks her daughter, her daughter says she only has five, and the age spots on her hand disappear and so do the wrinkles on her wrist, and look, there's Harry, her husband, who she would swear to you is dead, only he is much alive and she blinks her eyes and now she is down to four grandchildren, and she finally understands where this is headed, and that pretty soon she will meet her father again and she knows what that means, only this time it's not gonna happen, the nights of closet hiding and his footsteps at her bedroom door, and even if it means finding her mother, who is certain to pop up any second now, young and undementia'd, and trying to convince her that when she meets the man who will end up the father, to tear up his phone number, date any of the other boys, even if it means that the daughter will never be.

Next Thing She Knew,

It was spring. Still no sign of David. David of the stay right there. David of the nothing's wrong. David of the I need time to wander.

And so he wandered. Stories about him came back to her over casual chats. Know-it-all said, *I told you so.* Gossipy said, *I saw him with Christine.* Spiteful simply smiled, *good.*

Spring kept hanging around with its leafy canopy thing. Flowers and buds and such. She felt she ought to look. All this rebirth screaming *please have hope.* Then she'd go home to see if the phone had moved. If a call from David had somehow grown into her answering machine.

Next thing she knew, it was summer. Frosty lemonade. Air conditioner hum. Christine agreed to meet her for drinks. Comes in smiling. "Well, hello, Marie. Long time." Kiss, kiss. Christine tries to tuck in the cloud of *David Loves Me,* but it just keeps popping up out of the menu.

"Christine," she finally says, "you realize that instead of sitting here, we could be at the beach. If you would just let go, if you would just give me back my life, we could sit and hear the ocean's roar."

Christine nods and says, "yes, we could." She nods again. "We could, but we're not going to."

Next thing she knew, it was fall. Crackle and pumpkins and crunch. Thoughts of a new and better life poked her awake each morning. She started to think *possible, possible.* She learned again to match her shoes.

Of course, that's when David came back. Mumbled something about this and that. She only half-listened. *Christine was just* — and *you're the only* —. David hung around and fed her sweet juicy, apples. Soon she heard everything.

Next, of course, winter. She began to hear nothing. Not the snow heaving the roof, not her friends tip-toeing out of her life. One night, she thought she heard David whisper Christine in his sleep. She started to listen. Then she stopped.

Next thing she knew, it was spring.

THE CAKE, THE SMOKE, THE MOON

It is Fourth of July and the pop pop smoking the air, and the gray foggy fingers stretch way up into the humid night and dig down into the water. We sit there on the beach. We are lined up like questions. Where does smoke go when it dies?

One of us says we are children, and we don't need to know. Another of us decides it is time for cake.

We eat the cake and a third one says, we have to wait an hour now. She is the one who will follow the trail of the smoke fingers into the water. The water, that even an hour from now, will be lit up only by the moon.

The rest of us will wait safe on the beach, cake crumbs on the blanket. We will watch the water open its mouth and swallow. The one walking into the water, and looking for the smoke, will never find it, and we can only watch as she never pops her head up like a firework dud. The lifeguards run their useless legs into the water, and even the moon knows it's too late. And we sit and we sit, scooping up leftover cake crumbs, all of us knowing what's next.

DIVORCE STEW

When Ruth hears about me and Harry, she takes me over to *Rudy's Bar* and offers to make her famous Divorce Stew. "You'll love it, Marge. Potatoes and carrots, comfort stuff," she says. "Soon, you'll forget about that bastard."

"It was all my fault," I tell her, cause I know she will spread it all over town. "I had a secret lover."

She settles in like a hungry dog. "Ooh," she says, "I'm making you that stew for sure."

"And my lover," I whisper "wasn't a man."

I wonder how Ruth can sit so still and be jumping out of her skin at the same exact time.

"*Two* stews!" she says. "Tell me, who was she?"

"Oh, no one you know," I say, but with my eyes, I motion to Hannah, the knockout barmaid our husbands couldn't keep their brains off of.

I can see Ruth filling up, about to burst, and I put up 5 fingers, 3 times.

"15!" she yells, then slaps her own mouth shut when Hannah looks over at us.

I am a terrible liar. I just refuse to give Harry the upper hand. By morning, it will be all over town about me and Hannah, though to tell you the truth we have barely said hello.

All the men will wonder what I've got so special that even beautiful Hannah can't leave me alone.

I tell Ruth that I'll take her up on her offer of Divorce Stew. Then I sit back and look over at Hannah, who is acting oddly cool towards me. I shake it off and wait for my future of being wildly desired, which is going to start any minute now.

SUMMER STORY

Wet sand and seaweed gook. Tide creeping under your salt-bloated toes. Last night's bonfire ashes smoking towards the sky.

The beach house behind you is a slapdash of woodbones. Every so often a window. Open enough for airfingers to slip in and stroke someone lover-like.

And speaking of lovers — where did yours go? Last night, his full-moon face in the bonfire light, then later, hovering above you, behind you, under you.

Last night, he built a sandcastle. Then he showed you the sandcastle. Then he was the sandcastle.

You'll understand if he ever comes back. Just watch as the seafingers stroke him away at low tide.

THE MILLER'S BARBECUE

It is the night of the Miller's barbecue. End of August ritual. Everywhere, summer loves are shutting down. Sheets being draped over hearts like they are vacation furniture.

Mr. Miller, loan officer down at the bank, prods the burgers. They are nicely striped and ready to be turned.

Mrs. Miller glides through the yard with the same swimmy elegance she uses in their pool. Blonde hair and midriff top, she fills the glasses with lemonade.

Bret, the 19 year old neighbor, stares at her thighs. She pretends she doesn't see him. Pretends there were no late cricket nights in the garage while her husband slept.

While her husband dreamed about interest rates and garden tools and oh yes, Margaret. Margaret, who is right now waiting by the grill for her second burger and ends each conversation she has with Mr. Miller the same way, "when are you going to tell her?"

Bret rattles his empty ice cube glass towards Mrs. Miller, who is talking to Frank Brown. "I am thirsty," Bret whispers. And when she doesn't answer, he jumps fully clothed into the pool.

Where everyone suddenly stops what they're doing to watch this love-heavy boy sink straight to the bottom.

Everyone except Margaret, standing alone now by the grill, watching the burgers sizzle down to coal while Mr. Miller jumps in to save poor Bret. Bret, who flip flops like a landed fish once he is back on the concrete. And just as Mrs. Miller starts to look at her hero husband with an interest she hasn't shown in years, Margaret whispers into the burger smoke air, "you know, *now* would be a perfect time."

ABOUT THE AUTHOR

Francine Witte's flash fiction has been published in numerous journals and the anthologies *Flash Fiction Funny* (Blue Light Press) and *New Micro: Exceptionally Short Fiction* (W.W. Norton.) She is the author of two flash fiction chapbooks, *Cold June,* (Ropewalk Press) winner of the 2010 Thomas Wilhelmus Award, and *The Wind Twirls Everything (*Musclehead Press.) Her novella-in-flash *The Way of The Wind* (Ad Hoc Press,) was cited as a highly recommended selection in the Bath Flash Fiction Award. Her poetry chapbooks include two first-prize winners, *First Rain* (Pecan Grove Press,) and *Not All Fires Burn the Same* (Slipstream Press.) She is the author of two full-length poetry collections, *Café Crazy,* and *The Theory of Flesh,* (both from Kelsay Press.) Her play *Love is a Bad Neighborhood* was produced off-Broadway by Miller Coffman Productions. She edits the column *Flash Boulevard* on George Wallace's Facebook blog *poetrybay.* She is an associate editor for the *South Florida Poetry Journal.* She is a former high school teacher. She lives in Manhattan, NYC with her husband, Mark Larsen.